Built to Last

Tara L. Carnes

A Publication of The Poetry Box®

Poems ©2022 Tara L. Carnes
All rights reserved.

Editing, Book & Cover Design: Shawn Aveningo Sanders
Cover Art: Steve Johnson

No part of this book may be reproduced in any manner
whatsoever without permission from the author, except
in the case of brief quotations embodied in critical essays,
reviews and articles.

ISBN: 978-1-956285-08-6
Printed in the United States of America.
Wholesale Distribution via Ingram.

Published by The Poetry Box®, May 2022
Portland, Oregon
ThePoetryBox.com

For Emma, Kelly, and the Ward clan

"Fall seven times, stand up eight."
—Japanese Proverb

Through the voices of many survivors, these poems take a fearless look at domestic violence and the support systems that make it possible to heal from this trauma.

If you or somebody you know needs help—

National Domestic Violence Hotline:
1.800.799.SAFE (7233)
https://www.thehotline.org/

Contents

One
I Wonder	9
See's Candies	10
Christmas	12
When I Eat a Cobb Salad	13
Options	14
Girls' Night Out	15

Two
If You Tell	19
Leaving CPS	20
Now You See Me	21
A Day in Court	22
Maybe	23
My Ex Scared Me	24
Anamcara	25
The OK Charade	26
Mater	27
Ever This Night Be at My Side	29

Three
Fire and Gasoline	33
Held	34
Mending	35

After We Escaped to East Texas	36
Neighbors	37
Outside the Study Window	38
January 23rd	39
But They Don't Fall Down	40
Built To Last	41

Acknowledgments	45
Praise for *Built to Last*	46
About the Author	49
About The Poetry Box®	50

One

I Wonder

the saxophone collage still hangs on my wall
a goodbye gift
from the church choir to me
signed by all the members on the back

we sang and laughed together until you showed up
made me leave my party

shame on me
for trying to keep the peace
leaving with you

would my life have turned out differently had I said *NO?*

See's Candies

I clean the floor
and hear above me
the doctor's heels
    clicking
as she readies for work

she stopped by yesterday
with a box of
See's Candies
    her phone number
taped on top
she hears what is going on
    "do you need help?"

I didn't realize
she might have
    heard me
crying and crying
in the unfinished
nursery or throwing up
when his car drives in because
    I am so scared

I know now
she must have heard him
    screaming
"fat, bitch, stupid, cow"
    slamming me
into the walls

with my huge
    pregnant belly
I crawl around
scrubbing hardwood floors
on hands and knees
hoping that
    maybe
he won't get mad today

if the floor shines
the trash is
    not too full
his shirt hangers
    are spaced evenly apart
    and
I cooked the right meal

Christmas

a family get together
    smart clothes
    baking bread
    gift laden tree
    blaring football game

our baby cries in teething misery
he jams his fingers in her mouth
I protest "they're dirty"
he slaps me across the face

conversation stops—everyone freezes

"how about them Cowboys?" someone hoots
conversation resumes like nothing happened

When I Eat a Cobb Salad

it reminds me of my younger self
the twenty-something me
who played the saxophone
had so many dreams for the future and
ate cobb salads en route to band rehearsals

when I became pregnant
his abuse escalated
we left

I could not breathe deeply enough
to play my saxophone anymore
church gigs became a welcome second income
a better lifestyle
for a single mom
seeking a home

Options

when things get bad
no one notices
when I stay late at work
teachers do that

I practice piano for hours
at my church job
then sleep on crunchy old pew cushions
the sanctuary quiet

sometimes I stay with
elderly choir members across the street
through the blinds
we watch my ex
paw through the recycling bin
and stomp around our porch

my best friend's family
shield me too
and keep for me
an extra toothbrush and contact solution

Girls' Night Out

sisters by choice
we came together once a month
shared potluck and wine

supported each other
talked through
divorces, cancer
court battles
problems with kids, work, family
love and loss

gave as gift
laughter, tears
advice, honesty
trust and hugs

only once we tried to go to a movie
started crying near the end
cried all through the credits

when the lights came on
the theater ushers waited patiently
to sweep us out of the theater

Two

If You Tell

I'll KILL

    your cat

    your best friend

    your mom

    you…

There is no

evidence of abuse.

    The child

        won't

            talk.

Leaving CPS

White Christmas lights
smother the bushes
as we numbly
crunch to the car

The rejected pink bunny
she casts aside and
curls on the floorboard
hugging Teddy hard

She clutches his
disheveled, patchy fur,
breathing in the smell of this
familiar
faithful
friend

Scratched-up eyes that have
witnessed her abuse but
no mouth
so he can't tell
either

Now You See Me

he stalks me
relentlessly

nails in tires
peeping in windows
threatening phone calls
bicycle flybys
tidal waves of emails
    and texts

littering my car with his
"attorney at law"
business cards

parking in my
driveway
drinking Shiners and
leaving
empties on the porch

just in case...

    I
    didn't
    notice
    him

A Day in Court

incredibly personal
attorney/client conversations
swirl around
the freak show that is
family court hallway

when the judge enters
the courtroom
I'm lost in thought and realize
everyone is standing
     oh yeah, oh yeah
and jump up

my ex's lawyer opens with
fantasies and lies
"that's a bunch of crap -why would they say that?"
     (flies out of my mouth)

my lawyer glares and
punches me a reminder to shut up

waaay on up high
the judge restrains a smile

Maybe

maybe this doctor will help
    maybe...

or will their eyes just
show pity as they leave with
a quick turn of their back?

or will their mouths
twist in disgust,
spitting scorn on this
stupid mother?

or will they drop us
    like a
    HOT
    potato...scared of a lawsuit?

or will they say—
"I am retiring"
"your insurance is not valid"
"this is not my area after all"
"don't come back here if you suspect abuse"

standing outside myself,
    I wait...
too painful to observe,
so I look away—
    and so do they

My Ex Scared Me

enough to buy a gun
a patient friend
taught me to shoot

my hands shook so much
the shot patterns
skittered off
         the
              paper
                  targets

I took home his targets instead
human outlines with
the brains and balls
skillfully pierced in a shot pattern
the size of a quarter

I carefully
tucked them
in the recycling bin
with just a few tantalizing
      bits
           peeking
              out

my neighbor and I
watched through the blinds
that evening
as my ex snooped through
the bin (as was his habit)

the look on his face
when he pulled out the targets
priceless

Anamcara

"everything is going to be ok," you said
as you touched my hand

I am surprised

no one has **ever** told me that
not after they hear about my situation
most, in fact, avoid talking about it

I wonder what kinds of things
you have experienced
since my story doesn't scare you off

weeks, months, years, we talk

when I feel trapped and hopeless
you show me I have the POWER to choose
choose to run away
choose to stay and fight

I stay and you stay
accompanying me in the darkness
sharing your wisdom and faith
awakening my strength

The OK Charade

Fifth-graders bustle in
importantly dropping travel

toothpastes
    shampoos
        and soaps

into the box labeled "Women's Shelter"

As the guest speaker begins I
pin myself against the back bulletin board
hoping they don't notice my exhausted eyes
mismatched outfit and unwashed hair

My mind buzzes with questions

Will I ever escape him?
    Why is this happening?
        What friend will hide me tonight?

Shame and fear
hold this secret that
my students do not know

Their teacher IS a social awareness project

Mater

when things get really bad
I slip into chapel
and talk to Mater

curled at the end of the pew
in her quiet alcove
I feel safe

the hum of traffic
and the clatter of students
fades away

warm sunlight
streams through
the jeweled colors
of Mater's window

I love her pink gown
crown of stars
and the way her head is
bowed and listening

I close my eyes like hers

and know that
she understands despair

how it feels
to see your child
being hurt
and not being able to stop it

I beg her
again
please keep my baby safe
give me strength
to
hang
on

Ever This Night Be At My Side

Sitting in the rocker frozen
held breath, listening hard—
twitching
at the night's
skittering sounds

Does he know we're here?

lights out
phone unplugged
car parked elsewhere

        and baby sleeps on

Angel of God
my guardian dear, we
wait for his drunken footsteps

my fingers brush the
reassuring steel

breathe in
                breathe out

no sleep tonight

Three

Fire and Gasoline

my ex raged to the judge
said my best friend and I were like
"fire and gasoline"
when we were together

"explosive"

"dangerous"

"un sta ble"

my ex really hated the way she gave me

hope

courage

strength

to leave our abusive situation

to move far   away   from   him

before we left
our Girls Night Out group had a going-away party
posed for pics wearing T's
printed up with the words
"Fire" and "Gasoline"

Held

moving van long gone
heading to our new home, new life

settling the cat carrier into the crammed Saturn
B.J. howls
we drive away from a long
unbearable nightmare

after crossing the county line
emotions overwhelm
I never thought we would see this day
a giant leap of faith into uncertainty

I cry and cry for miles—B.J. howls
tears of joy and relief
held in the Divine's embrace

Mending

months
after we arrive I
remind myself
    and marvel
that we are safe here
        we are safe

so many emotions
years of bad memories
for years shut off
like a light switch

    but now

feelings rush through me
    a faucet
turned on full blast
this fire hose torrent
of sadness and fear

only time
can slow this deluge
    to a drip
        drip
            drip

After We Escaped to East Texas

friends helped us put a mobile home on their land
my ex mocked us "you are *such* white trash!"
we decided to own it
"we are *not* white trash—we are *fancy* white trash!"

for our first Fancy White Trash Party
drew on sharpie tattoos
pulled together crazy, sketchy, outfits
(I wore my "one size fits most" muumuu)

dined on tea party delicacies
cucumber sandwiches, chocolate chip scones
sweet iced tea served properly on china

neon yard flamingos glowed
resale shop candles flickered nestled among garden rocks

in celebration, we laughed and danced to Roma music
the dark forest embraced us

Neighbors

pineywood bark
black and slick
under a
soggy, somber sky

frogs creak
jumping through
puddles and streams
of sandy water

on the porch
wrapped snug
in blankets
we eat
hot, spicy gumbo
with fluffy rice

and share
troubles and joys

Outside the Study Window

spring breezes rustle leaves
a clear, blue sky rejoices
today is Easter Sunday

I sit and feed a few pages at a time
into the hungry shredder…grind…grind…
tedious, loud, yet satisfying

stacks and stacks of your legal refuse
that you churned out for years
trying to control us…grind…grind…

I smile as legal letterheads
are pulled into the spinning jaws
mashing and crunching up painful memories…grind…
   grind…

a red light pops on
overheated…
wait 30 minutes

a new strength fills me
when the last pages are eaten up
we are overcomers…grind…grind…grind…grind…

January 23rd

The caged bird sings with a fearful trill of things unknown but longed for still and his tune is heard on the distant hill for the caged bird sings of freedom.
—Maya Angelou

ten years ago today
this miracle occurred

our Emancipation Day
from you
from your abuse

leaving everything familiar behind
we leapt out in faith
trusting the Divine to catch us

traveling slowly through the
spiral of transformation
cycling through grief
reliving dark paralyzing fear
tingling pricks of feeling awaken

healing by
sharing our story
moving beyond our story
hearing others' stories

as survivors, we soar
no longer victims encaged
each day growing
stronger and bolder
singing our song of freedom

But They Don't Fall Down

my ex sent me a drunken email
at 2:08 a.m. and copied our judge

he called me a "Weeble"
(among other things)
for my refusal to stay down
after repeated legal punches

I printed a picture of Weebles®
and glued it to
my heroes-poster-collage where

Ghandi walks
Rosa Parks sits
Malala speaks
Mother Teresa touches
Corrie Ten Boom hides
MLK marches
Sacajawea leads
Joan of Arc charges
Hildegaard sings
Nelson Mandela forgives
Crazy Horse fights
Julian of Norwich guides
Philippine Duchesne teaches
Joan Chittister preaches
Arab Spring protesters shout
Burmese Monks challenge
D.C. Mayor Browser paints

BLACK LIVES MATTER

and a lone Chinese student
stares down a tank
in Tiananmen Square

Built To Last

The words you speak become the house you live in.
—Hafiz

    I took
    the disparaging words
    others had
            flung
    at me

    repeated and repeated them
    made them my own

    built this house
    of selfdom
    a brittle shell
    scraped and dented by
           these internal voices

    the shingles took
    a beating of
    rapid fire hateful words
          fat –bitch-stupid-cow
    which seeped in and
    dripped
         down
            the
                rafters
    into a dark
    spidery
    pool of
    untold stories and secrets

    moldy wisps of mutters and sighs
    repeat "you are unlovable"

[. . .]

half-rotted
stair steps alternate
           stupid -ugly
                   stupid-ugly
                           stupid-ugly
waiting to collapse
my self-confidence

"you will never amount to anything"
slithered in the murky sink water
           unable to escape
down the clogged drain

a weary ceiling fan
whispered
"now look what you've done"
leaving undisturbed a thick
layers of dusty
"you don't belong here"

closet doors
stuffed with put-downs
spilled out
           "whale"
           "klutz"
           "ugly"
           "four-eyes"
           "loser"

but
when you know better,
you do better and
with help
I struggled to stop this
litany of self-hatred
this soundtrack of malice

I learned to put
good thoughts out
into the universe and
 look at myself in the mirror
and say "I love you"

            slowly, slowly
an orange glow of hope
bravely shone through the
cracked, dirt-smeared windows
of my soul

mantras of
        "you belong here"
        "you deserve this"
        "you are loved"
        "you are beautiful"

restored and updated
this weathered and wise sanctuary

the bones of this abode
now stand strong
a must-see remodel
with an excellent view
            of the future

Acknowledgments

Special thanks to The Haden Institute's Cathy Smith Bowers, who taught me about the abiding images in poetry, and Diana McKendree, who first encouraged me to submit my poems for publication.

Heaps of gratitude to all the friends, family, neighbors, co-workers, and helpers who were sent by the Divine to encourage and sustain us through many difficult years.

Grateful appreciation is given to Shawn Aveningo-Sanders and Robert Sanders at The Poetry Box, for shining a light on this difficult topic.

Thank you to the editors of the following publications where some of the poems in this chapbook first appeared:

> *Cholla Needles Magazine*: "Christmas," "January 23rd," "Maybe," "Now You See Me," and "The OK Charade"
>
> *Ilya's Honey:* "Built to Last"
>
> *Presence: An International Journal of Spiritual Direction:* "But They Don't Fall Down"
>
> *Prometheus Dreaming*: "My Ex Scared Me"
>
> *SageWoman Magazine*: "See's Candies"
>
> *The Very Edge Poems* (Flying Ketchup Press, 2020): "Options" and "Mater."
>
> *Voices de la Luna*: "Ever This Night Be at My Side" and "Leaving CPS"

Praise for *Built to Last*

In language as precise as it is restrained, Tara Carnes' *Built to Last* is a testament to Carl Jung's theory of the individuation process—that process each of us must move through in order to become the human beings we were intended to become. Carnes shines a vivid light on scenes of shame, despair, abuse, and terror and on scenes of courageous attempts to help others who have experienced the same. Despite the physical and emotional traumas these poems explore, Carnes shares with us those moments when she has finally taken ownership of her power, enjoying unabashedly her comeuppance. Always, though, at the core of this trilogy of suffering and survival, there is a deep reverence for those both Divine and earthly who have journeyed with her *in the darkness/ sharing [their] wisdom and faith.*

—Cathy Smith Bowers
Poet Laureate of North Carolina 2010-2012

Domestic abuse victims hide their bruises. Their stories gen-erally remain hidden—unspoken and unwritten. Fear. Fear will take a voice. Fear will do that.

This collection of poetry empathically speaks their truth. And more than their truth, it records their hard-won transformation from victim to survivor. Grit. Grit will keep you alive. Grit will do that.

Survivors have a voice. They unapologetically tell their stories with the hope of giving strength to those who follow. Courage. Courage will give a voice. Courage will do that. This. This is what they know.

—Ingrid Knox

I am struck by the number of sensory nouns Tara uses in this compilation of poetry. It stands to reason, since it's about domestic violence, which we feel, touch, taste, smell, hear.

The horrible words directed at us, the smell of a Teddy bear who brings solace, the taste of a salad which reminds us of times we felt safe, the touch of a friend's hand or our head resting on our arms in the presence of Mary as a girl. The feelings: terror, fear, anxiety, worry, embarrassment, shame, self-blame during the time of entrapment, and, conversely, feeling the joy of freedom and the freedom of joy, the capacity to breathe deeply and laugh from the belly (and play the saxophone, once again), the freedom to cry the tears of leaving (not the tears of waiting for him to come home to torture), the strength to de-program one's self from all that was dumped into us and on us by our abuser(s).

Tara also uses many present progressive verbs, which suggests to me that the process of recovery from domestic violence is not a once-and-for-all event; rather, recovery happens over time, in time, during experiences that recapitulate the original abuse, through conversations with friends who love us, and in the silence of being in the heart of Creation.

You cannot read this poetry and not be affected by it. May it affect you and help you commit to intervening when you witness domestic violence or are told about it by someone you know.

—Mary Kay Hunyady, RSCJ, PsyD

Tara Carnes delivers poetry with a punch in *Built To Last*, her collection of poems about the nightmare that is domestic violence. Carnes presents a picture of broken hearts and broken dreams by drawing honestly and unflinchingly on survivors' struggles to escape abusive partners. At times sad and disturbing, at others hopeful and even funny, Carnes recounts the realities and hurdles an abused woman, especially one with children, faces in a society where everyone would just as soon *Not Know*. Instead of giving in or giving up, Carnes relies on her own keen determination and the support of devoted friends to change her life and to ensure a future for herself and her daughter.

Built To Last is not an emotionally easy read, but it is an immensely worthwhile one. Carnes packs so much into each poem; one read is not enough. She skillfully makes use of poetic form and style to convey unsettling images that have multiple depths of meaning. Tara Carnes shares the stories of courageous survivors in *Built To Last*.

—Linda Weiland

About the Author

Tara L. Carnes is a musician, writer, teacher, and spiritual director. She has an MA from the University of North Texas and spent over thirty years working as a music educator and church musician. In 2012, she began writing poetry as part of her coursework for the Haden Institute (Niagara, Ontario) spiritual direction program.

She loves using the rhythms of words to embrace both the dark as well as the light in her work.

Besides tough issues such as domestic violence, she writes poetry about nature, spirituality, and motherhood and utilizes them in her spiritual direction practice. Brené Brown stated, "When we deny our stories, they define us. When we own our stories, we get to write a brave new ending." Tara looks forward to many years of sharing her experiences, and "living a brave new ending" through the music of poetry!

Tara's poetry has appeared in *Snapdragon: A Journal of Art and Healing*, *SageWoman*, *Cholla Needles*, *The Poeming Pigeon*, and *The Very Edge Poems* (Flying Ketchup Press). She lives in Texas with her daughter and their handsome, plush, tuxedo cat, Orion.

<http://www.taralcarnes.com/poetry>

About The Poetry Box®

The Poetry Box, a boutique publishing company in Portland, Oregon, provides a platform for both established and emerging poets to share their words with the world through beautiful printed books and chapbooks.

Feel free to visit the online bookstore (thepoetrybox.com), where you'll find more titles including:

Erasures of My Coming Out (Letter) by Mary Warren Foulk

Of the Forest by Linda Ferguson

Sophia & Mister Walter Whitman by Penelope Scambly Schott

Dear John— by Laura LeHew

A Shape of Sky by Cathy Cain

A Long, Wide Stretch of Calm by Melanie Green

What She Was Wearing by Shawn Aveningo Sanders

The Catalog of Small Contentments by Carolyn Martin

Tell Her Yes by Ann Farley

Contraband by Juan Pablo Mobili

Just the Girls by Pamela R. Anderson-Bartholet

Beneath the Gravel Weight of Stars by Mimi German

A Nest in the Heart by Vivienne Popperl

and more . . .

www.ingramcontent.com/pod-product-compliance
Lightning Source LLC
LaVergne TN
LVHW020442080526
838202LV00055B/5313